2023

During my journey in healing, I had to dig deep down inside and really analyze myself. There were moments of self-reflection, criticism, doubt, and confusion but it was necessary to face all of this and re-evaluate the chosen paths. I will admit that shit was rough! Excuse the language but this is real life, uncut dialogue.

chipped

ADJECTIVE

1. damaged by having a small piece broken off at the edge or on the surface:

bro·ken

1. having been fractured or damaged and no longer in one piece or in working order.

A LETTER TO MY FIRST BORN

Hey son,

 I want to start this off by first saying thank you for playing a major role in who I am today. You chose me as your mother just at the right exact moment, when I needed to know what unconditional love was. I was in the middle of going from one toxic home to another unknowingly, searching to fill the void of masculine love. I heard that if your first born is a boy, that's God's way of giving you that unconditional love that has no strings attached, no expectations…. just pure love. You have grown up with me and been by my side through all my ups, downs and in betweens. Yet you still never judged me, and you love your mama regardless! I thank you for my beautiful grandchildren and for you being the best father you know how to be. I pray that you receive an abundance of peace, happiness, wisdom and favor. I pray that God grants you all your heart desires and discernment to sustain. I love you son, my A1 from Day 1.

With love,

Mom

A LETTER TO MY BABY BOY

Hey son,

I want to first thank you for choosing me as your mother so that you can teach me patience and determination. You received the unhealed version of me and for that I apologize. Your unwavering love, even through my pain, kept me going. Your ability to never give up on me or anything you do inspired me to become the best version of myself and I am appreciative. I thank you for where we are today and just know, it's only up from here baby!! I pray Gods hands to cover all of you and anything you go after. I pray for an abundance of clarity, peace, strength, wisdom and discernment to carry you through. I pray God orders your steps and you continue to shine and succeed! I love you son, my Super Star, I will forever be your #1 fan.

With love,

Mom

THIS BOOK IS DEDICATED TO MY SUNSHINE,

MAY YOU FOREVER R.I.P.

LISA R. SMITH-ROLLINS

8/9/1968 – 4/9/2024

"I LOVE YOU CUZ, KEEP WATCHING OVER YOUR "ANGEL"

PROLOGUE

I am sharing my experiences to encourage others to do the same. There is this ugly stigma that therapy is bullshit and for crazy people. We are so caught up on what others think that we fall into that box and never seek the help that we need. This literature is for anyone that may have wanted to seek professional help or even just seek personal help in their life. But I wrote this specifically with women in mind, we must bear so much. We not only carry ourselves but our children, our men (that are tore down from just living every day), our parents and sometimes just the kids in the neighborhood. The fact that women are natural nurturers we are expected to help everyone. Speaking from my own experiences, I would always take on so many projects because deep down I needed to help myself, but I chose to run from it. I have always attracted or been drawn to people that have similar traumas to myself. Once that connection happens, I put my all into trying to save them when all I was doing was losing myself and needed saving. I have been running from my inner self since childhood. I was conditioned by my parents to act like everything is ok and not to talk about problems (especially household business) I know many of you can attest to the famous phrase "what goes on in this house stays in this house". But with me going to therapy I was forced to look at my life thus far and work on each piece to rebuild Me. Yes, I was a mess, but with time and dedication, I am getting it together. We must be careful with the words we allow to exit our mouth. The words we speak daily are very powerful. Get out of the habit of calling yourself broken. If something is broken, then there is no more use for it. If something is broken, you toss it in the trash, dispose of it. So, if anything, say you're chipped. Yes, we all have flaws or may not be feeling our best, but baby you can and will be repaired. And until you are in fact repaired, you are still worthy! Pick your head up and go full speed ahead! I consider myself Chipped And NOT Broken because I am working progress. Within the book I am telling my story and allow the reader to think about how it may relate to them. For me writing about my obstacles helped me to be able to talk about them. Once I say it out loud, I'm ready to tackle it head on. So come along my journey as I tell you about the many pieces of me, flaws and all......

A LETTER TO MY YOUNGER SELF

Dear NaKeisha,

Don't ever lose yourself trying to "win" someone else! Stay true to you and you will never doubt your worth. You can do whatever you set your mind to do. Stay focused on your goals and reach for the sky! Always believe in yourself and love you first. Never compromise your peace and sanity trying to please others, trust me, it never works out. Just relax and enjoy every moment that you are granted. People come into your life for a reason, a season or a lifetime. So, appreciate those people who you encounter for however long. Cherish those experiences because they will make you into who you are intended to be. I know you're saying "yea right" …. but please believe me, everything that you're going to go through will be a lesson or a blessing and sometimes both. As I close this letter, I want you to remember that you can't love someone else if you don't love yourself first. People can only love you to the level they know. Once you understand that you will handle life and relationships better. I am proud of you, and I love you! You will be happy and you're going to love it there!

Love,

Future Me

IF YOU LOOK INTO MY LIFE & SEE WHAT I SEE...

This is a powerful phrase, and it resonates all through me. This exact act is very necessary if you want to properly heal. The one thing that I found to be the hardest to do is evaluate myself. How many times have you found yourself judging others and having opinions about someone else and what they have going on? It's so easy to do that, but as soon as we must look at ourselves in the mirror to play judge and jury with our own shit, we get lackadaisical. Speaking from experience, I don't want to hear others' opinions about myself, so I sure didn't want to give myself the business. But let me tell you.... this is very necessary, and I suggest everyone to do this at some point in their life. When I decided to embark on my therapy journey, I really didn't know what I wanted or why I wanted to start. Looking in hindsight, I was running and letting someone else tell me something was wrong with me and had me believe they knew me better than I knew myself. And they didn't know me at all, hell, I didn't even know me. Once I realized that "I" needed to make a change, I set my plan into action, but still treading lightly. To prepare for my journey, I chose to make a list of things that I wanted to change about myself. This was me trying to figure out if I was going to get the help, I knew I needed but kept running from it. That was hard because who really wants to focus on what needs improvement, let alone pick those things out yourself. This list was one of the toughest, most stressful moments in my life, and writing down on paper what my flaws were AND speaking about them out loud, caused many emotions to surface.

WHAT ARE 3 FLAWS YOU WOULD LIKE TO WORK ON?

1. _____
_____
_____
_____

2. _____
_____
_____
_____

3. _____
_____
_____
_____

flaw

[flô]
NOUN
flaw (noun) · **flaws** (plural noun)
1. a mark, fault, or other imperfection that mars a substance or object:

THE LIST......

- Communication – listening to understand and not to respond.
- Insecurity – knowing who I am and what I am capable of
- Trust – learning how to trust others to do what they say they will do.
- Acceptance – accept the things that I have no control over
- Submit – allow someone else to lead.
- Apologize – willingly apologize when necessary.
- Petty – stop tic for tac. No need to hurt others because I'm hurt.
- Be vulnerable – let down my guard and show my vulnerability and transparency.

5/12/2021 – This list was created when I decided that I wanted to seek therapy. I wrote down the obstacles that I was allowing to stand in my way of healthy relationships. When I say relationships, I mean which includes family, intimate, and platonic. The way I was moving was so unhealthy and I was in denial as many of you can relate to, I'm sure.

THE ASSIGNMENT

My very first assignment from therapy was to create a timeline of my life as far back as possible of things of significance from childhood to adulthood. Although I went back as far as 4 years old, I had gaps in time. I was instructed to read through my timeline while in session #2 and as I was going down memory lane, my therapist would ask me questions. The questions would then have me think of a response and I then gave a quick answer. In real time I didn't know what she was doing or trying to tell me without telling me. At the end of my appointment, I heard some things that really brought me to an "aha" moment. There were very significant events that I placed on my outline that I just kind of shrugged off as if it was no big deal. Things that were very monumental I acted as if it was just ordinary things. I also realized that I skipped things, and this is just a defense mechanism that I created so I won't have to deal with emotions. To me, minimizing my issues to make them not important was what I would convince myself to do, because someone else is going through something bigger and I would focus on that. By holding onto emotions with no proper outlet it made me very guarded and defensive. Which in turn caused a great deal of turmoil in my life. I would not want to show my weakness, by crying or talking about what was bothering me. I recently read a quote that said something to the effects of, "crying doesn't indicate that you are weak. Since you were born, it's always been a sign of you being alive". That right there speaks volumes! That itself lets me know that perception is everything. We learned that crying is a weakness when in fact it is very beneficial. It's a way of cleansing, soothing yourself by shifting your mood, and just a release of tension, stress and help regulate your emotions.

On a separate piece of paper, construction board or even in a journal, complete a timeline of your life. Write down events and then go back to each event and think back to that time and come back to this page and write down emotions you remember feeling. You can use this list to reflect on how you deal with certain situations emotionally and change the result if necessary.

- _____
- _____
- _____
- _____
- _____
- _____
- _____
- _____
- _____
- _____
- _____
- _____
- _____
- _____
- _____
- _____
- _____
- _____

A DAUGHTER'S 1ST LOVE

This is where it all started. I always heard that a father is his daughter's first love. In the past I believed that was a lie, however, looking in hindsight I see that was true for me. Look at the "men" I chose All of my past partners have been like my dad and that choosing was done unconsciously. They all had some type of addiction (my dad's was alcohol), all had a violent streak and controlling (whether physically, or emotionally). Although I didn't like how my father treated my mom, I loved him immensely!

Daddy Issues:

All my life I have yearned for undying love and attention. Now my father was indeed present in my life, but he just didn't know or understand how to give love properly. Although I was his "Angel face" I can't even tell you what it felt like to receive a hug, a dance, a one-on-one conversation or even a simple I love you. I loved my dad and just wish I could say I knew he loved me too. I remember always wanting to be around him as a little girl. He would ride me on his 10-speed bicycle down to Cobbs Creek Park and play tennis with his friends. On the ride he would sing my song to me that he made up when I was born {Angel face, you got that pretty little angel face} Yes there were some good times, but they always ended as bad times. My dad was my first interaction with toxicity. Of course, I didn't know this at that time this is my self-diagnosis. This has been a great roadblock for me and I just kind of suppressed it and searched everywhere high and low for that unconditional love that I know I longed for. I, just like many others, looked for love in all the wrong places, I know it sounds cliché but that's as best that I can describe it. I looked for love in my kids, in men and friends. I have been searching for 45 years and have just realized that I must love myself wholeheartedly so that the love can be poured into me correctly and from the right people.

To be honest I was looking for something that I had no real experience in……being loved properly. Growing up I had to witness domestic violence more than I'd like to admit. My mother did everything to be the perfect wife/mother but still it was not "enough". She would get us ready for school, clean the whole house, wash clothes, have dinner ready, then bathe and get dressed by 4 pm every day. She did this so that when my dad came home, she looked like she had just stepped off the runway and so he would be at peace. Needless to say, that peace would only last as long as a case of beer.

Me being the "baby" of the family, I would try everything imaginable to make my daddy happy just so he wouldn't get upset and take it out on my mom. I would try to make him laugh by telling jokes or playing the "who sing this" game (my dad loved music and swore he could sing) or running back and forth to the refrigerator to bring him another beer. Little did I know that as I'm bringing him the beer it was only making him more and more intoxicated so was that really making him happy? I remember going to sleep every night and praying hard that when I woke up, I wouldn't have to see my mom bruised and sad. As I got older and was able to really grasp what was happening at home, I became very withdrawn, confused, angry and helpless. This was very traumatizing growing up in this kind of environment and not being able to tell anyone. All I could think of was….is this love? I tried very hard to never put myself or my children through this type of lifestyle, however with me looking to be loved caused me to disregard many "red flags" in relationships. I reasoned with myself and justified this by thinking at least they weren't beating on me. I stayed in relationships longer than I should have. I absolutely love "LOVE" and just wanted someone to love me. There were times that I knew the guy I was dealing with wasn't really "all in" but he told me what I wanted to hear. This is what is now called love bombing. Which is nothing but someone who shows you all the attention and care one moment (to most likely get whatever it is that they want from you) and then turn cold on you when they've gotten what they were needing at that time. In my mind it was ok because at least I wasn't getting beat down every day. But I was getting beat down, I accepted abuse at some level in each relationship. Now it may not have been as extreme as what I witnessed as a child, but it was still abuse. Abuse can be physical, verbal, emotional, financial and mental as well. None of it is acceptable and if you are experiencing ANY form get away immediately. You deserve to be treated correctly and with love and care.

This mentality took a toll on myself and my children, so I wasn't creating a healthy environment for my sons either. I couldn't tell you what love is, but I knew what love wasn't. Family love and affection was something unfamiliar to me in my own household. The closest thing to it was sitting in the living room watching scenes from The Cosby Show play out on the TV screen.

A lot of adults today suffer from daddy issues and may not even know it. Society has taught us that only females experience the trauma from daddy issues but as I sit back and think it can be both females and males that this epidemic takes a hold of. And contrary to what we think brings on "daddy issues", it's not just from not having a "2" parent home. I for one can attest that I grew up in a two-parent household and still at the age of 45 am haunted by daddy issues. Although my father lived in the home and provided financially for my mother, siblings and I, he wasn't present. Let me explain…….my father went out to work five days a week, Monday-Friday and brought home the bacon so that my mom, who was a stay-at-home mom, could cook it up. He was excellent at providing financially, however, there are many other things that were lacking such as love, affection, quality time. I grew up watching great tv shows of black families that showcased fathers interacting with their children, especially their daughters and I wanted that so bad. I couldn't even tell you how many times I've heard my dad say "I love you" to me or my siblings. This is what I believe has led me to have such a hard time making proper choices in men. As soon as I would get "the attention" I was all in, all gas and no brakes. I instantly connected that attention with love and would take whatever nonsense that came with it. One huge impact of my daddy issues is that I would date, and even marry once, the same person repeatedly. It may have been a different face and name but the same attitude and mentality. You may relate that to as being "my type". Let me tell you that my type sums up as: have served time in prison, has mommy issues (anger/resentment), can't love themselves, unstable finances, and looking for a place to stay. I programmed myself to think that I didn't need a man due to watching my mom. She depended solely on a man to take care of her, and he didn't value her. This was very painful to watch as a child. I vowed to never depend on anyone, let alone a man. For me being with a guy who didn't have more than or equal to me was ok in my head. For him to need me but I didn't need him gave me a sense of empowerment. In a twisted way I felt like it was payback for how man treated my mom. I wanted to always be in control because there was no way in hell a man was going to tell me what to do.

I grew up being shown that love was pain by witnessing and hearing the beatings of my mom and siblings, and the phrase that I despise is "I'm doing this because I love you". If anyone tells you that I suggest you head for the door, because love DOES NOT hurt. Love is a beautiful thing and will never hurt.

There are many types of abuse, and it does not have to be physical and show visual marks or signs. Listed below are commonly found in relationships:

- Physical Abuse: any form of physical force or violence inflicted on a partner, such as hitting, punching, kicking or restraining.
- Emotional/Verbal includes behaviors aimed at controlling, belittling, or manipulating a partner's emotions through verbal attacks, insults threats and humiliation
- Psychological: involves manipulation of a partner's thoughts, feelings and behaviors through tactics like gaslighting (making them doubt their own reality), mind games and intimidation
- Sexual: non-consensual sexual acts or coercion, including rape, unwanted sexual advances, sexual humiliation, or withholding sex as a form of punishment
- Financial: controlling or exploiting a partner's financial resources, such as restricting access to money, withholding financial information, or preventing them from working or accessing education
- Digital: using technology to control, monitor or harass or intimidate a partner, such as constant texting, tracking their whereabouts via GPS, hacking into their accounts or spreading rumors online
- Isolation: deliberately cutting off a partner from their support network, such as family and friends, to increase dependence and control
- Spiritual: exploiting or distorting religious or spiritual beliefs to justify control, manipulation or mistreatment within the relationship
- Stalking: persistent and unwanted attention or surveillance, both online and offline, that instills fear and threatens the safety of a partner
- Neglect: failing to meet a partner's basic needs for food, shelter, safety, or emotional support, leading to physical or emotional harm

Recognizing these forms of abuse is crucial for individuals to seek help and support to break free from unhealthy relationships and establish boundaries for their own safety and well-being.

National Domestic Violence Hotline 24/7

(800)799-7233

A CHILD LEARNS WHAT THEY LIVE

Growing up my siblings and I weren't taught or shown familial love which I believe is of top tier importance. It shapes us as we grow into adults. We didn't learn how a man is supposed to properly love his wife, we didn't learn how to love our siblings and we damn sure didn't learn how to love ourselves. Now that we are older, we have learned these skills by retraining our thinking through trial and error. By that I mean we are all products of failed marriages and out here in our 40's and 50's still trying to get love right. My siblings and I have shown our children different and give them the love we desired growing up. I gave them hugs, talked to them and kept open lines of communication; tell them I love them as often as possible. Even now that they are grown and have busy lives, I will send a text randomly to let them know I love them or send an affirmation or a motivational clip. I do truly admire how our children love each other and now their children, our grandchildren, share that same bond and expressions of love. At least we were able to change the dynamics and show our children a different upbringing in that respect.

ACTIVITY:

- What are ways that your childhood household helped or hindered you?

  _____

  _____

  _____

  _____

- Are you raising your child/children the same way?

  _____

  _____

  _____

  _____

- What actions have you taken or will take to ensure you are teaching your child/children about healthy relationships?

  _____

  _____

  _____

  _____

  _____

CO-DEPENDENCY

This was a tough subject for me to speak on. It was just recently during my journey that I understood what that word means. I would always be in denial when that word was thrown at me. I mean I would get downright offended if anyone ever referred to me as such. Thinking I don't depend on anyone for anything! Period! I have always worked since I was 14 years old and provide my own wants and needs very well, thank you. My definition of co-dependency was to depend on other people to take care of me financially. However, that is not the total gist of it. My new way to define it is leaning on someone to provide whatever it is that you are craving or needing at that moment. In my past relationships, I was depending on them to bring me happiness and to love me and that was a big no-no. Can't nobody or nothing bring you happiness other than you. Happiness is created within and pours out. You must love you first that way you won't have to search far. I read somewhere that codependency is the neglect of self to gain approval, love and self-identity from someone else. Ouch! That one sentence gave me such clarity. That sums it up in a nutshell. This is the act of losing yourself when you're in a relationship. You get so entangled in the life of your partner or your children that you no longer have self-knowledge. You put your all into them and wait for them to give you kudos. If this sounds familiar, then you got to shake that off! Look at this list to give yourself an assessment.

***** *I do not have any medical background and cannot make any type of diagnosis. The lists/charts that are provided in this book are purely for "self-evaluation" and "self-awareness".*

codependency

[ˌkōdəˈpend(ə)nsē]

NOUN

1. excessive emotional or psychological reliance on a partner

AM I CODEPENDENT?

Lack of trust	
Anger	
Dependent on others	
Controlling	
Caretaking	
Repression	
Obsession	
Denial	
Disconnected self	
Relationship problems	
Weak boundaries	
Sex issues	
Poor communication	
Need for approval	
Shame and doubt	

TRAUMA BONDING

A lot of my intimate relationships were built on the most troubling feelings. It wasn't love or even lust, it was feeling connected to that person based off what we've been through that seemed so familiar to each other. When getting to know someone you will talk for hours asking questions about their upbringing, family, and different life events. How many times have you had conversations and will say "oh wow! Me too!"? At that moment you form a connection and get so excited that finally someone "gets" me and understands me. This can be a great thing, but most often it just stirs the pot and creates a molehill of turmoil.

Trauma bonding in relationships often results from intense emotional experiences and prolonged abusive or manipulative behaviors. This bond forms not from love, but from shared traumatic experiences, which causes us to become deeply attached to our abusers. Understanding the effects, recognizing the signs and learning how to heal from trauma bonding is crucial in breaking free from its chokehold and reclaiming your emotional well-being.

Effects of trauma bonding in relationships:

- emotional intensity: trauma bonding promotes increased emotional force, creating an addictive pattern in the relationship. Things like abuse, manipulation, and fear become entangled with moments of kindness and affection. The up and down spiral of emotions keeps the victim psychologically hooked to the abuser.
- Submissive and dependency: victims of trauma bonding often develop a sense of helplessness and dependency on their partner. The balance of kindness and manipulative tactics instills a belief that their well-being and self-worth are solely determined by the partner's approval.
- Isolation: abusers commonly isolate their victims, cutting them off from sources of support. This isolation prevents the victim from

seeking outside perspectives on the relationship, further ingraining the trauma bond.

- Self-blame and guilt: trauma bonding often causes you to internalize the blame for their abusive circumstances. You may believe you deserve mistreatment, leading to guilt and shame. This perception makes it tough to recognize the abusive dynamics and seek help.

Recognizing Trauma Bonding:

- Induced helplessness: take note if you feel trapped, powerless, or unable to make decisions without your partner's approval or involvement.
- Inconsistent relationship patterns: recognize if your relationship goes between moments of intensity, love, and kindness, followed by abusive, controlling or manipulative behaviors.
- Isolation from support: evaluate if you have been isolated from your friends, family, or any support system, leaving you solely dependent on your partner for support and validation.
- Fear of leaving: notice if you experience intense fear, anxiety, or a sense of loss at the thought of leaving the relationship, even when it appears harmful.

Healing From Trauma Bonding:

- Seek professional help: reach out to therapists or counselors experienced in trauma recovery to help you gain clarity, identify patterns, and develop coping strategies.
- Rebuild Support Systems: mend connections with friends, family or support groups.
- Educate yourself: self-educate by reading books, attending workshops, or joining support groups focused on trauma bonding and its effects. Look for groups on social media.

Understanding the dynamics can empower you with knowledge to break free.

- Develop self-compassion: shift blame from yourself to the abuser. Practice self-care, self-love and forgiveness. Engaging in healing activities such as meditation, journaling, and therapy can help in rebuilding self-esteem and reclaiming personal identity.

Healing from trauma bonding is a difficult but essential journey towards reclaiming freedom, self-worth and emotional well-being. By understanding the effects of trauma bonding, recognizing its signs and seeking professional help and support, individuals can heal and break the vicious cycle.

TRAUMA BOND	AUTHENTIC CONNECTION
EXPLOSIVE, INTENSE FROM THE START, FLUCTUATES CONSTANTLY	GRADUAL PROGRESSION TOWARDS GREATER INTIMACY
"I NEED YOU", "I'M ADDICTED TO YOU"	"I SEE YOU", "I HEAR YOU"
CHAOTIC, UNPREDICTABLE, A ROLLER COASTER OF EMOTIONS	PREDICTABLE, SAFE, MUTUAL TRUST, WORDS ALIGN W/ACTIONS
EMOTIONALLY PHOBIC, BUT HIGHLY SEXUAL	EMOTIONALLY VULNERABLE, OPEN COMMUNICATION
RESCUING, ENABLING, SAVING EACH OTHER	LEARNING, WITNESSING, EVOLVING TOGETHER
FEAR OF ABANDONMENT	WORK TO CREATE SAFETY W/EACH OTHER
BETRAYING YOURSELF & NEEDS TO BE CHOSEN	HONOR OUR OWN NEEDS/LIMITS AND EACH OTHERS
KEEPS SCORE, USES INTIMATE KNOWLEDGE AGAINST EACH OTHER	CURIOSITY, ACCEPTANCE, ABILITY TO HOLD SPACE FOR EACH OTHER
EMOTIONAL ADDICTION TO EACH OTHER/FEAR OF SEPEARATION	PREDICTABILITY, SECURITY, PEACEFULNESS THAT CAN FEEL "BORING"

A REASON, A SEASON OR A LIFETIME

People come into your life for a reason, a season or a lifetime. We just have to ask for discernment so that we know which time frame is presenting. How many of us try to hold on to relationships even though we can see or feel that things are going left? We just want to keep hope alive because we feel a sense of loyalty to this person, or we are too afraid to be alone, or we worry about what people will say if I leave this relationship. You better stop being scared to refresh that screen on this thing called life. No matter how long people are in your circle, enjoy every minute and appreciate the experience.

I am very loyal to people I allow into my life. I want to hold on for dear life and will go above and beyond to keep my friends and partners even if I'm hurting myself by doing this. There's a phrase that says, "God protects fools and babies" and believe me when I tell you He has never let me down. At times when I could not walk away God has always stepped in and removed those people for me. I'm not a baby but have played a fool one too many times! I have struggled with this my whole life and am currently working on the act of detachment. Being attached to "people" makes you be so wrapped up in them and their feelings, emotions and energy that we begin to absorb all of that like a sponge. We lose ourselves trying to hold on to them and expecting them to act a certain way or treat us a certain way. By being able to detach we open ourselves up to unlimited possibilities and allow life to just flow naturally.

A MESS

Hurt people hurt people……that is a phrase that I never could agree with. What I believe is, hurt people attract hurt people. By this I mean that we often get with individuals that we feel attracted to and don't even realize that the attraction is merely a reflection or "trauma attraction". Trauma attraction is when people come together feeling like you have a lot in common because of similar upbringings or experiences. Looking back, I can see my pattern of always getting with individuals that I felt like I could fix. And that's not just in romantic relationships, I gravitate towards anyone that I saw needed some type of fix. After being able to look into myself I believe that was just me crying out for help for myself and not acknowledging it. I was and am always looked at as the one who can handle anything, the one that seems like they have it all together. Just because you see me smiling doesn't mean that I am happy. My smile was just a mask that I learned to wear very early in life.

But with therapy I have finally been able to rip that mask off and face my biggest opponent, me! I am a working progress and very proud of the person I have become and anxious to see the person I will be. I have acquired skills to heal from within and would love to share with everyone who is unsure of where to start. It's all about sharing love one person at a time. My journey so far has had me on an emotional rollercoaster, but I am so grateful for the experience. I have learned to love, encourage, motivate, and advise myself. If I can't do those things for myself, how can I expect it from someone else or even do those things for others? I used to think that taking time out for "you" was selfish especially if you are in a relationship or have children. But it's not, that is necessary, and I encourage you to do it. Take yourself on a date or go get a manicure and pedicure, pamper yourself and I guarantee you will feel such a euphoric feeling just by indulging in self-love. Set aside some time in the week where you do 1 thing special. You can start small to get into the habit. I like to get a pedicure and sit in that massage chair and just enjoy the moment with my earbuds in with some meditation music. Make a list of ideas you would like to choose from to spoil yourself. You deserve it!

- _____
- _____
- _____
- _____
- _____
- _____
- _____
- _____
- _____
- _____
- _____
- _____
- _____
- _____
- _____

Self-love (n) regard for one's own well-being and happiness.

Self-care is vital for maintaining mental, emotional, and physical well-being. Here are some self-care practices that are amazing for beginners:

- Establish a routine: Start by setting time aside each day for self-care activities. This could be a few minutes for meditation, exercise, reading a book or taking on a hobby.
- Prioritize sleep: Make sure to get enough sleep each night. Try to sleep at least seven hours to recharge and rejuvenate your mind and body.
- Do deep breathing exercises: Take a few moments throughout the day to focus on your breath. Inhale deeply through your nose, hold it for a few seconds, and exhale through your mouth. This trick helps ease stress and promote relaxation.
- Physical activity: Start with something as simple as going for a walk or trying a beginner's yoga class. Doing this can boost your mood and improve your overall well-being.
- Have a nutritional diet: Be sure to incorporate healthy foods, vegetables, and fruits for a nice balance.
- Disconnect from technology: Take breaks from screens and social media. Dedicate time for music therapy.
- Practice mindfulness* or meditation: Consider adding mindfulness or meditation to your daily routine. These practices can help you develop a greater sense of awareness, reduce stress, and promote relaxation.
- Set boundaries: Learn to say no when necessary and establish healthy boundaries in your personal and professional life. This will help prevent burnout and maintain a healthy work/life balance.
- Engage in activities you enjoy: Simply put, make time for hobbies and activities that bring you joy. Whether it's painting, dancing, cooking, or playing musical instruments, doing things you love will impact happiness.

- Seek support: Don't be afraid to reach out to others for support. Talk to friends, family members, or seek professional help if needed. Sharing your thoughts and emotions with someone can provide relief and support during challenging times.

Remember, self-care is a personal practice, so feel free to explore and experiment with various activities to find what works best for you. Start small and gradually build on these practices to develop a sustainable self-care routine.

*Mindfulness is simply just being fully present, aware of where we are and what we are doing, and not overly reactive of what's going on around us. You can do this seated, walking or standing. Just embrace the moment!

MEDITATION

Meditation is a practice that involves training your mind to focus and redirect your thoughts. It is often used to improve mental clarity, reduce stress, and enhance overall well-being. Here's a simple explanation for beginners:

Meditation typically begins by finding a quiet and comfortable space where you can sit or lie down. You can choose to close your eyes or keep them slightly open, whatever feels more comfortable for you. The goal is to be in a relaxed state.

Start by bringing your attention to your breath. Observe the natural rhythm of your breathing, feeling the air entering and leaving your body. Focus on the sensation of your breath without trying to control it. If your mind wanders, gently guide it back to your breath.

As you continue to meditate, you may notice an influx of thoughts, emotions, or sensations arising. Instead of getting caught up and trying to overanalyze, just acknowledge the presence and let them go. This is called non-judgmental awareness. Try to be in the present moment, without reading too much into the past or worrying about the future.

Gradually, you can explore different techniques. Some beginners find it helpful to count their breaths, repeating a mantra, or visualizing calming scenes (this helped me tremendously). These techniques provide a focal point to anchor your attention.

Remember, meditation is not about having a particular outcome or having a completely thought-free mind. It's about creating a non-reactive and non-judgmental awareness towards your thoughts and experiences.

I recommend starting with short sessions, like 5-10 minutes a day, and gradually increasing the time as you build up your confidence. It's all about consistency and discipline with this, and quality over quantity. Once you are comfortable with meditation it will help you develop a greater sense of peace, focus and clarity in your everyday life. Once I got into it, I would look forward to that time and also began to know when my body needed it. I personally use YouTube to guide me, and I recommend this for you. The video will guide you and walk you through step by step as you learn how to do it solo. You can search for specific things that you need clarity with. There is no right or wrong way to use meditation. You can sit upright, with legs crossed, laying down even in the tub. It's all about relaxing and clearing your mind. You also have an option to meditate as you sleep, I have noticed that I sleep better and wake up more refreshed. If you try this technique, use the space below to reflect on your experience.

_____
_____
_____
_____
_____
_____
_____
_____
_____
_____
_____
_____
_____
_____
_____
_____
_____
_____

ALPHA FEMALE/ALPHA MALE

This is the strong woman that a lot of "men" are intimidated by. These "men" often will try to convince you that being strong and direct is bad, but I'm here to tell you that you are dealing with the wrong man. This is how society try to dictate how we as women are to carry ourselves and enough is enough. An alpha female is a woman who can lead, knows her worth and not afraid to lay down boundaries and if that's too much "masculine energy" for you than sorry, not sorry. I have learned to embrace myself and love me for who I am. I oftentimes would dumb down myself to satisfy the ego of the man I was with and now I realize that was not my issue to deal with. If my partner is not comfortable with my resilience, then is he truly a partner? Your significant other should never be ok with you not being your absolute best, in fact they should be helping you bring it out. It takes a true alpha man to embrace, accept and understand an alpha woman. To know the strength of that title personally is the only way to comprehend it. What man wouldn't want a strong woman as their partner in life? Although I consider myself to be an alpha female and have always had that "no nonsense, I'm standing on business" attitude in my relationships I feel like I can be submissive for the right MAN. Being the head of the household has always been on me (even during my marriage). I was the worker, it was my house/apartment they moved into, and I made the decisions. Part of this was because I conditioned myself to not depend on a man so he could never control me from witnessing my mom go through this. Trying to recover from that way of thinking is extremely challenging. I am ready to be in my soft girl era, I want to ride in the passenger seat sometimes! Healing is a lifetime process, there is no such thing as "healed" because you will always be tested. We are human so no matter how much we think we have gotten over something, it's going to come back around. Will we pass the test? Not every time and that is perfectly ok! As long as you recognize it, you have the opportunity to do what's best for you and get it right.

BE IMPECCABLE WITH YOUR WORDS......

This phrase was introduced to me this past year. When I first heard it, I didn't quite grasp it truly. I was intrigued by the meaning behind these five words. What does it truly mean? Our words can be a beautiful dream or an ugly nightmare. It can build something up or tear it down. With that being said practice on yourself, on being impeccable with your word by looking in the mirror and say these affirmations:

- I am beautiful inside and out.
- I will have a great day on purpose and in my purpose.
- I am confident.
- I am projecting the energy that I wish to receive.
- I am exactly where I need to be at this moment in time.
- I am ready to love and to be loved.

Now feel free to come up with a few of your own:

- _____
  _____
- _____
  _____
- _____
  _____
- _____
  _____

I CHOOSE ME

Instead of crying to another sad love song,

I CHOOSE ME

Instead of wondering and questioning where I went wrong,

I CHOOSE ME

Instead of fighting for a love that don't love me,

I CHOOSE ME

instead of settling for far less than I deserve,

I CHOOSE ME

Instead of sacrificing my happiness,

I CHOOSE ME

When it comes to my peace....

My sanity......

I

CHOOSE

ME!

Made in the USA
Columbia, SC
29 July 2024

39033107R00024